WITHDRAWN

World of Reptiles

Cottonmouths

by Matt Doeden

Consultants:
The Staff of Reptile Gardens
Rapid City, South Dakota

Capstone press

Mankato, Minnesota

Bridgestone Books are published by Capstone Press,
151 Good Counsel Drive, P.O. Box 669, Mankato, Minnesota 56002.
www.capstonepress.com

122009
005643R

Library of Congress Cataloging-in-Publication Data
Doeden, Matt.
  Cottonmouths / by Matt Doeden.
      p. cm.—(Bridgestone books. World of reptiles.)
  Includes bibliographical references and index.
  ISBN-10: 0-7368-3730-2 (hardcover)   ISBN-13: 978-0-7368-3730-9 (hardcover)
  1. Agkistrodon piscivorus—Juvenile literature. I. Title. II. World of Reptiles.
  QL666.O69D634 2005
  597.96'3—dc22   2004014480

Summary: A brief introduction to cottonmouths including what they look like, where they live, what they eat, how they produce young, and dangers cottonmouths face.

Editorial Credits
Heather Adamson, editor; Enoch Peterson, designer; Ted Williams, cover designer; Erin Scott, illustrator; Jo Miller, photo researcher; Scott Thoms, photo editor

Photo Credits
Ann & Rob Simpson, 16
Bruce Coleman Inc./John Shaw, cover; Joe McDonald, 1, 4; Daniel Lyons, 20
Corbis/Joe McDonald, 18
Pete Carmichael, 12
Tom Stack & Associates Inc./Joe McDonald, 10
Visuals Unlimited/Rudolf Arndt, 6

Table of Contents

4

Cottonmouths

Cottonmouth snakes swim through swamps hunting fish. Cottonmouths kill **prey** with deadly **venom**. They are dangerous **predators**.

Cottonmouths are reptiles. Reptiles are **cold-blooded**. Reptiles also have scales and grow from eggs.

Cottonmouths belong to a family of snakes called pit vipers. All pit vipers have small holes, or pits, below their eyes that sense heat. The pits help them find prey. Rattlesnakes and copperheads are also pit vipers.

◀ Cottonmouths can swim with their heads out of the water, watching for prey.

What Cottonmouths Look Like

Cottonmouths have thick bodies. Most adults are 3 to 4 feet (0.9 to 1.2 meters) long. Tan and brown scales cover their bodies in a stripelike pattern. The scales usually grow darker as they age. Older cottonmouths sometimes look black or green.

The name "cottonmouth" comes from the white color inside the snake's mouth. The snake looks like it has cotton in its mouth. A cottonmouth opens its mouth wide to scare away predators.

◄ Cottonmouths open their mouths and show their fangs to scare off predators.

Cottonmouths Range Map

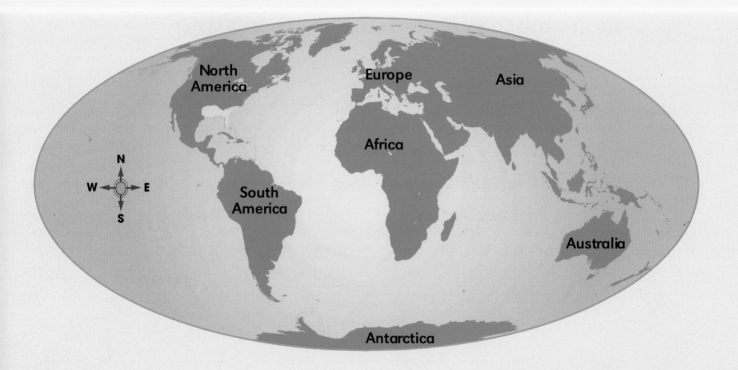

North America

Europe

Asia

Africa

South America

Australia

Antarctica

☐ Where Cottonmouths Live

Cottonmouths in the World

Cottonmouths live only in the southern and southeastern United States. They live in the wetlands and swamps of Florida, Louisiana, and parts of Texas. They can live as far north as Virginia, Kentucky, and southern Illinois.

◀ Cottonmouths live only in the United States.

Cottonmouth Habitats

Cottonmouth habitats are near water. They often live under rocks or logs that lie alongside the water. Cottonmouths can swim with their heads out of the water. They hunt animals that live in swamps, rivers, and lakes.

Cottonmouths that live in cooler places **hibernate** in winter. They leave the water to find warm dens. In the spring, they return to the water.

◀ Cottonmouths spend most of their time near water watching for prey.

What Cottonmouths Eat

Cottonmouths mainly eat water animals. Their prey includes fish, frogs, and small turtles. Cottonmouths sometimes eat birds, lizards, and even other snakes. Some cottonmouths eat small alligators.

Cottonmouths use their heat-sensing pits to find prey. They then use their fangs to deliver poisonous venom. The venom causes the prey to bleed inside its body. Cottonmouths swallow prey whole.

◄ Frogs are a common meal for cottonmouths.

Life Cycle of a Cottonmouth

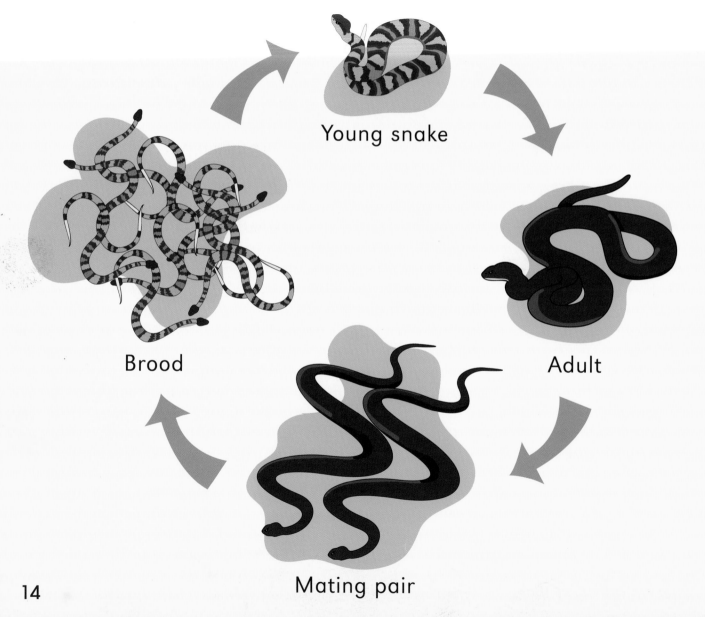

Young snake

Adult

Mating pair

Brood

Producing Young

Cottonmouths **mate** in early spring. A female carries her young in thin egg sacs inside her body. She gives birth to the live young three or four months after mating.

A female may have up to 12 young at a time. The group of young snakes is called a brood. A newborn cottonmouth is about 8 to 10 inches (20 to 25 centimeters) long.

Growing Up

Young cottonmouths are ready to live on their own at birth. They use their tails to hunt. The tips of their tails are brightly colored. They shake their tails to attract small fish.

Young cottonmouths grow quickly. Cottonmouth skin doesn't grow as the snake grows. Instead, cottonmouths **molt**. They shed their old skin and uncover new skin.

◄ Young cottonmouths move their yellow tails like worms to attract prey.

Dangers to Cottonmouths

Cottonmouths have few predators. King snakes and large birds, such as hawks or herons, kill cottonmouths. Largemouth bass may eat young cottonmouths.

Cottonmouths are not at risk of dying out. People rarely build homes or roads in the swampy areas where cottonmouths live.

Cottonmouths are dangerous. The snake's strong venom gives people a good reason to stay away.

◀ A red-shouldered hawk eats a young cottonmouth.

Amazing Facts about Cottonmouths

- Doctors use **antivenin** to treat people bitten by cottonmouths. This medicine is made from venom. Without antivenin, a person can die within hours of being bitten.
- People often mistake water snakes for cottonmouths. Water snakes are usually harmless to people.
- Some people call cottonmouths "water moccasins." Moccasin is an American Indian word that means "to wrap around."

← Doctors take venom from a cottonmouth's fangs to make antivenin.

Glossary

antivenin (ant-ee-VEN-in)—a medicine that reduces the effects of snake venom

cold-blooded (KOHLD-BLUHD-id)—having a body temperature that is the same as that of the surroundings; all reptiles are cold-blooded.

hibernate (HYE-bur-nate)—to spend winter in a deep sleep

mate (MATE)—to join together to produce young

molt (MOHLT)—to shed an outer layer of skin; cottonmouths molt several times as they grow.

predator (PRED-uh-tur)—an animal that hunts other animals for food

prey (PRAY)—an animal that is hunted for food

venom (VEN-uhm)—a poisonous liquid made by some snakes; snakes inject venom into prey through hollow fangs.

Read More

Barnes, Julia. *101 Facts about Snakes.* 101 Facts about Predators. Milwaukee: Gareth Stevens, 2004.

Feldman, Heather. *Cottonmouths.* The Really Wild Life of Snakes. New York: PowerKids Press, 2004.

Internet Sites

FactHound offers a safe, fun way to find Internet sites related to this book. All of the sites on FactHound have been researched by our staff.

Here's how:
1. Visit *www.facthound.com*
2. Type in this special code **0736837302** for age-appropriate sites. Or enter a search word related to this book for a more general search.
3. Click on the **Fetch It** button.

FactHound will fetch the best sites for you!

Index